# Breaking the Silence: Saving Young Lives from Mental Health Struggles

***The Critical Guide to Understanding Childhood Pain and Preventing Tragedy***

**Copyrights**



**Legal Disclaimer!**

This book is authored for informational and educational purposes only.

While the publisher and author have made every effort to provide accurate information, they make no representations or warranties of any kind, implied or express, about the reliability, accuracy, completeness, availability, or suitability of the contents for all persons.

The reader assumes full responsibility for the use of the information contained herein.

The publisher and author disclaim all liability for any damage, loss, injury, or expense that may manifest from the use of the information contained in this book.

# Foreword

Modern life is truly a stressful one and its impact affects children and teenagers the most: mental health is a shadow crisis. ***Breaking the Silence: Saving Young Lives from Mental Health Struggles***– a carefully crafted guide, written with passion and rigor to help parents, teachers, and caregivers identify, understand, and provide solutions to the mental health issues young people face.

Currently, Nabila Kauser has been using her kindness and understanding words to finally make people aware of the suffering of children. This book is not a political pamphlet or rallying cry, it is a guide to make change on a much larger scale. I do not think there is an encouraging statement about today's society from shattering the silence and shedding light on the stigmas that children and adults alike must endure to letting children have the tools that they need to succeed academically, emotionally, and mentally.

This book is a present – to all those people who want to stand firmly for change, sustain, and be empowered in order to be able to impact the lives of youngsters.

# Dedication

For each child in this world who has experienced hearing the cruel words of 'nobody wants you,' or being on the receiving end of a dismissive adult who didn't see you, this book is for you. Your problems are important, your voice is important and you have a right not only to live but to enjoy your life.

In this book tribute, I hope that the parents who lose sleep tossing and turning because their child's battles remain invisible and silent and the caregivers who tirelessly try to bring comfort and hope, your love shines and guides the healing.

To the teachers, mentors, and supports out there who know that a positive word, a listening ear, and an open heart—you who are building a better tomorrow – Thank You.

For every worker in the mental field, who spends their lifetime, working on child suffering, your empathy and devotion truly ignite the possibility of change.

And to those people who decide to go public about the disorders they go through in their day-to-day lives, this is for you: Your bravery sets waves of change that the subsequent generations will continue to absorb.

This book is dedicated to all of you. Collectively we can create a future where every child will be accepted, encouraged, and can freely succeed.

# Acknowledgments

This would not have been possible without the support and inspiration of many incredible individuals:

- To the children and families who tenebrously told their stories, thank you for the stories you told me. It's for those who are brave – your courage is the core of this exercise.
- To my fellow professionals practicing in the mental health field, your input and expertise contributed to the creation of this book in so many instances.
- To my family – my source of strength and inspiration for choosing the noble cause of actively pursuing the wellbeing of children – thank you.
- To all the readers who take this book with the aim of bringing change– you are the hope that our children require.

No longer shall we tolerate silence hence, breaking the silence.

# Preface

As this paper will further elucidate, that mental health is the foundation of a child's health and should as such not be overlooked or understudied as it currently is. In our society, excellence can be measured by scores in school and the ability to fight the physical battle of life while the emotional fight of the children is kept hidden.

***Breaking the Silence*** is actually a result of an understanding that all children need to be listened to and supported. It is passionate work that is based on research and personal experience as well and it provides tools when it comes to the need to determine such signs and intervene appropriately for the sake of the caregiver as well as create emotionally strong individuals.

Table of Contents

# About This Book

**Breaking the Silence: Saving Young Lives from Mental Health Problems** is a pioneering study of the unseen mental health epidemic in our children. Compassionately written and based on research, this book will try to expose to the light the secret burdens of the young and give readers the information and the means to save lives.

In a world overwhelmed by stress, technology, and social pressures, children often carry emotional burdens they cannot express. This book breaks down complex mental health challenges into accessible insights for parents, teachers, caregivers, and anyone involved in the well-being of children.

With in-depth insights, firsthand experiences, and practical tips, *Breaking the Silence*, exposes symptoms of mental health problems, underlying causes of psychological distress, and the heartbreaking effects of undiagnosed problems. It also outlines a way forward for prevention, intervention, and building a protective context in which children will feel emotionally safe to talk about their feelings.

This isn't just a book—it's a mission to create a world where every child's mental health matters. Away from the book, this is a potent call back to the fact that we are all in a position to change a child's destiny. A call to action for communities to come together and protect the youngest among us. By breaking the silence, we can build a brighter future for children everywhere.

**Inside this book, you'll discover:**

- The detection of the early warning signals of mental health problems in children.
- Strategies used to intervene and support children when they are struggling.
- Resources for developing resilience and emotional health in children.
- Realistic practice abrogates the stigma of mental illness and fosters open dialogue.

- Insights into advocating for systemic changes to prioritize children’s mental health.

No matter if you are a parent, teacher, or just a person like us dedicated to change, this book will provide you with the ideas and knowledge required, to understand and change a child's mental health journey.

# Introduction

Mental health problems of children have become extremely high in recent years. The psychological health and well-being of children have become an increasing concern of parents, teachers, practitioners, and society in general. The pressures of modern life, coupled with a lack of education and resources for addressing mental health issues, have led to a troubling rise in mental health challenges among children, with many feeling hopeless and isolated. Several children experience profound emotional and psychiatric distress even culminating in suicidal thoughts and behaviours. However, often these challenges are hidden or left uncared for, making them worse.

Mental health disorders in children are not only a private or family matter but are a societal problem that demands urgent action. Mental health is certainly no less relevant than physical health, but has been undervalued and misunderstood throughout history. If we fail to give sufficient attention to the mental health of children, we risk their health and happiness on a long-term basis and their ability to flourish in the world.

Quite a few of the attentional health problems of children are unrecognized because of the stigma of mental illness. Young children rarely have the tools and vocabulary with which they can accurately describe their emotions, and when they do, they may be afraid of being rejected or scolded. Therefore, parents, carers, and teachers may not notice the first warning signals that are indicators of a severe psychiatric disorder. When these struggles are ignored or brushed off, the consequences can be severe. Children can resort to unhealthy ways of coping such as the use of drugs or self-injury, and they can also seem to ward off their suffering (depression, anxiety, suicidal ideation).

However, there is hope. There is increasing awareness and understanding of mental health problems in children, which, when appropriately treated, can be controlled and prevented. The solution to tackling this crisis lies in creating a climate in which children can talk openly about their feelings and challenges, identify symptoms early of mental health difficulties, and provide them with the means and support that will enable them to manage and flourish.

This is a plea from society's parents, caregivers, educators, and towards the health of children's minds as a whole, for action. It addresses the origin of the mental health epidemic in children, presents the clues of children who are having a hard time, and suggests intervention and prevention methods. In each chapter we will also cover how to challenge stigma in mental health, enable children to self-regulate their emotional states, and push for a wider systemic societal shift to guarantee children's access to mental health services whatever their background.

As we get more into a discussion of mental health issues in children, we should remember that mental health problems reflect rather than indicate weakness, but the enormous pressures these children are dealing with in an ever more complicated world. If we take these challenges on full-stop, we can ensure that children get the emotional regulation skills they need to deal with life's vicissitudes and become emotionally healthy, successful adults.

By publishing this book, we would like not only to raise awareness but to offer tools and actions that can be implemented to better the mental health of children. The purpose of this paper is to provide information and resources to parents, teachers, and caregivers of children with mental health issues with the aim of tangible contributions to improving the lives of children experiencing mental health symptoms. Work needs to be done to untangle the causes of these problems, acts of intervention as early as possible, and make sure that every child has a chance to grow up well, emotionally competent, and content.

When we begin this journey, it is worth remembering that mental health is not simply a personal matter and it's a social one as well. The health of children is directly related to the health of our society. If we, working in partnership, help overcome the barriers that silence is built on and ensure that the right support is there, we can make a world where every child has the opportunity to develop emotionally, mentally, and physically in a positive manner.

In the following chapters, we will discuss in which way this vision can be achieved. We will consider what cautionary signals parents and carers should look out for, we will consider what the underlying causes of mental illness in children are, and we will consider the value of early intervention. We will also discuss methods for developing emotional resilience, overcoming the stigma that surrounds mental health, and fighting for systemic transformation.

Our ultimate aim is to provide a detailed map for parents, caregivers, and educators to utilize when trying to provide psychological support for the young people living in their care.

The path to providing support to children's mental health is a road paved with empathy, insight, and action.

It's a journey worth making for our children's sake, for the sake of our communities and our future. Let's begin the conversation and work together to create a healthier, more supportive environment for children everywhere.

# Chapter 1: Mental Health in Children

Mental health is a key element of overall health and it is basic to children's thinking, feeling, and behaving.

Mental health can no more be isolated from physical health than can be overlooked in childhood development — it is integrated into every single aspect of a child's life, from their affect to social interactions, learning, and physical health. However, mental health has traditionally been a topic of neglect when we talk about child development in comparison to physical health.

Comprehending mental health in children is an important prerequisite for tackling the increasing prevalence of mental health problems in youth. As are physical health conditions, like asthma or diabetes, mental health problems are genuine and can have serious consequences for a child's life if they are not treated. But unlike physical disorders, mental health problems in children are more difficult to recognize, of a lower incidence, and that it is easier to ignore.

In this chapter, we discuss what mental health is about children, all of the factors that contribute to such an emotional/psychological state of the child, and the distinction between normal emotional growth and when there may be indicators of mental health difficulty. It is imperative to gain insight into the basis of mental health in the child population so that we then are in a position to effectively deal with the challenges that they are experiencing.

## Defining Mental Health in Children

Mental health in children is defined as the emotional, psychological, and social functioning of children that enables them to manage daily life stresses, develop positive interpersonal relationships, and achieve their maximum potential. Mental health impacts the way children approach, process, and behave in different contexts, such as within the home, school, and in their peer environments. It also modifies their responses to stress, and how they interact with others and make choices.

The mental health of the child is affected by different factors viz., biological constitution, family background, social interactions, and the cultural context in which the child lives. For healthy mental development in children, a complex interaction is seen between emotional regulation, social competence, and critical thinking and problem-solving. Children with healthy mental functioning are well-equipped to build relationships, manage everyday stresses, find enjoyment in activities, and manage age-appropriate adversity.

But just as an adult, they may have mental health problems. These can range from anxiety, depression, and eating disorders to more severe issues like obsessive-compulsive disorder (OCD), schizophrenia, or post-traumatic stress disorder (PTSD). Mental health disorders may impair daily life in a child, such as at home, in school, or interaction with others.

## Developmental Stages and Mental Health

To have a complete comprehension of the development of children's mental health, attention must be paid to how mental health problems are expressed throughout different developmental stages. The child develops over infancy and adolescence in physical and affective ways. Mental health problems may vary significantly according to the age of the child, and it is important to know what is normal in terms of emotional and cognitive development to know when there is a problem.

## Infancy and Early Childhood (0-5 years)

During the early years of a child's life, the foundation for mental health is being laid. Infants form emotional attachments with their primary caretakers and their emotional growth is intimately related to how they attach to their primary caretakers. During this period, the child depends on them for emotional control and security. Adaptive attachment experiences promote brain development of healthy brain and emotive resilience.

Nevertheless, neglected, inconsistent care or early trauma in infants or toddlers can have a deleterious effect on their emotional development. Signs of developing mental health in infants and toddlers can range from over-fussy crying to poor sleep, a lack of bonding with caregivers, generalized irritability, and difficulties making social attachments.

## Childhood (6–12 years)

When children enter the school-age years, their capacity to speak, think, and interact with the world increases. Mental health issues may become more apparent during this stage, as children face new challenges such as schoolwork, peer relationships, and increasing social pressures. It's also a time when children begin to develop a stronger sense of self and become more aware of their emotions and how they relate to others.

Typical mental health problems of this age group are anxiety disorders (e.g., separation anxiety), depressive disorders, attention-deficit hyperactivity disorder (ADHD), and behavior disorders. Children could exhibit signs of unhappiness, temper, or withdrawal, or could have problems with school, lack of focus, or difficulty listening. They may also face difficulties in establishing/maintaining friendships, and this can result in a sense of isolation or loneliness.

## Adolescence (13–18 years)

Adolescence is a time of dramatic emotional and psychological development. Teens undergo hormonal alterations that influence affect, identity, and relations with peers and family. They start to develop a stronger sense of who they are, their values, and their position in the world. This is a time of adventure, risk-taking, and heightened emotional experience.

In many adolescents, mental health problems can worsen, for example, depression, anxiety, eating disorders, self-harm, and even suicidal thoughts. Emotional dysregulation can be exacerbated by peer pressure, preoccupation with body image, academic stress, and yearning for autonomy. Teenagers could be experiencing identity problems, suffer from losing self-esteem, or become emotionally detached from family, and from the one with whom they do the most socializing. Possible signs of mental health disorders in adolescents can be mood swings, changes in behavior, social avoidance, or indications of extreme stress.

It is also worth to underline that the onset of some mental health disorders including schizophrenia or bipolar disorder is standard to happen during adolescence. For this reason, this phase is decisive for the detection and treatment of mental health problems at an early stage, before becoming more deeply embedded and hard to treat.

## Factors That Influence Mental Health in Children

In the mental health of children, things do not happen in isolation. It is conditioned by several interacting factors in intricate, multidimensional ways. These factors include some biological and some environmental.

## Biological Factors

Genetics are central to the mental health of a child. Children who have a family history of mental health disorders may be at an increased risk of developing similar conditions. E.g., depression, anxiety, and bipolar disorders have been known to exhibit a heritable component. Neurochemistry, stress processing and response in the brain, and the basic structure and function of the brain can also affect the mental health of a child. In some instances, impaired neurotransmitters or other biochemical influences may be involved in the emergence of mood disorders and other psychiatric diseases.

## Environmental Factors

Environmental factors play an important role in the development of a child's mental health. Emotional well-being is influenced by various factors, such as their home environment, school experience, and social interactions. A supportive family environment that promotes open communication, healthy emotional expression, and positive coping strategies is one of the most protective factors in a child's mental health. On the other hand, children who go through neglect, abuse, or lack of emotional support are prone to mental disorders.

Peer relationships are critical in childhood and adolescence. Bullying, exclusion, or negative social interactions can lead to feelings of insecurity, anxiety, and depression. On the other hand, deep friendships, and positive peer relationships such as can offer children emotional support, raise self-image, and foster resilience.

## Trauma and Stress

Trauma is one of the major risk factors for the occurrence of psychiatric disorders. Childhood trauma whether it be physical abuse, sexual abuse, emotional neglect, domestic violence, or exposure to community violence—can have lasting effects on a child's emotional and psychological health. Post-traumatic stress disorder (PTSD) is prevalent in children exposed to severe trauma, and they may present symptoms, e.g., flashbacks, nightmares, inattention, hypervigilance, and emotional blunting. Even experiences like the death of a loved one, divorce, or moving to a new area can create stress that impacts a child's emotional health.

Chronic stress, maybe with family problems, school staff, or social pressures, can also lead to mental health disorders. Children experiencing background stress may develop anxiety, depression, or problem behaviors. Caregivers should also be able to recognize the symptoms of stress in a child and then intervene to resolve the root of the problems before they exacerbate more serious MHP disorders.

# Chapter 2: Early Warning Signs of Mental Health Issues in Children

As a parent, caregiver, or teacher identifying a child's mental health risk signs in the early years is one of the most important steps to prevent deeper problems in later life. Early identification and intervention have the potential to greatly diminish the impact and ongoing ramifications of many mental health issues so that children can be given the care they require which will enable them to develop emotionally and socially. Sadly, mental health problems in children are too frequently misdiagnosed, misinterpreted, or ignored because of insufficient awareness, stereotypes, and stigmas about mental illness.

In this chapter, we will explore how to identify the early warning signs of mental health struggles in children, what these signs might look like at different stages of development, and how to differentiate between normal emotional fluctuations and more concerning patterns of behavior. Getting these signs early can make the difference between getting the attention a child needs and falling through the cracks.

## The Importance of Early Detection

The earlier a mental health complication is diagnosed; it is easier to treat and control. Psychiatric disorders are frequently chronic (i.e., they continue to deteriorate over time without medical management). Early intervention has the potential to avoid the progression of emotional and psychological problems and could prevent the development of more serious conditions, such as chronic depression, anxiety, or suicide.

Children also may not have the emotional lexicon and the emotional maturity necessary to verbalize their emotions effectively, making it difficult for parents or guardians to know when things are amiss. Moreover, mental health symptoms of children can differ from those of adults and it is therefore crucial to identify behavioral changes, mood changes, or unusual physical symptoms that could be a sign of an underlying mentally ill condition.

Although each child is an individual, some underlying patterns of behavior or emotional distress can be indicative of a psychiatric disorder. Such warning signs may appear immediately or over time and may differ in a child's age and developmental level. Efforts to identify that which is to be sought, and to take the initiative to get it, can reassure parents, carers, and teachers that children will be afforded early help.

# Signs of Mental Health Issues in Younger Children (Ages 3-8)

For children and young people, mental health problems can be particularly challenging to identify given a lack of verbal ability to provide for expressing their thoughts and experiences. Adolescents and young children are still developing their ability to modulate emotions, so their reactions to stress or discomfort can look like everyday tantrums, irritability, or behavioral difficulties. Nevertheless, if there are persistent or worsening patterns, they may serve as a sign of a latent mental disorder.

**Emotional and Behavioural Changes**

1. **Excessive Fear or Worry**: Children who are constantly anxious, fearful, or worried—especially about things that are not typically feared by others their age—may be experiencing anxiety. This might manifest as extreme clinginess, fear of being separated from a parent, refusal to go to school, or an overwhelming fear of certain objects, people, or situations.

2. **Regression in Behaviour:** A child previously displaying developmentally normal behavior may begin to regress to earlier phases of development. For example, they may begin to exhibit behaviors such as thumb-sucking, bed-wetting, or demanding a bottle, even though these were the behaviors they had outgrown.

3. **Severe Irritability or Outbursts:** Although some tantrums or outpouring of emotion in toddlers are not unusual if a child often exhibits extreme irritability, anger, or extreme rage for seemingly silly or nonsensical reasons when a child is prone to clinical, frequent, extreme irritability, anger or rage without apparent trigger, might indicate an underlying emotional or behavioral disorder. When such blushes happen repeatedly and are excessive for the situation, it might suggest a mood disturbance or malfunction in the regulation of emotion.

4. **Social Withdrawal:** A child who all of a sudden stops socializing play, who is not interested in games with peers, or who ceases to spend time with family may be experiencing an episode of

depression or anxiety. They may not be able to verbalize their feelings but the symptoms of withdrawal and absence of interest in things they used to enjoy will be manifested.

5. **Excessive Sensitivity:** A child who is unusually sensitive to criticism or seems to have low self-esteem may be experiencing anxiety or depression. They could experience intrusive thoughts, emotional overwhelm, and a perpetual fear of being rejected or failing.

## Physical Symptoms

Anomalous physical symptoms are not a priority in mental health disorders, yet signify a serious alert in children. Emotional distress can manifest as physical complaints, which children may not understand or be able to link to their mental health.

1. **Frequent Complaints of Physical Pain**: Pain, headache, or any unexplained somatic symptoms that recur over periods can often be ascribed to emotive distress. Anxious or depressed children can manifest psychosomatic symptoms such as

these, which can in turn impose limitations on their capacity to function properly.

2. **Changes in Eating or Sleeping Habits**: Uncontrolled episodes of out-of-the-blue changes in eating behavior including, failing to consume, overeating, or rapid weight loss or weight increase which could indicate psychological problems. For example, sleep disturbance as manifested by a heavy burden of nightmares, insomnia, or nocturnal wakening can suggest anxiety and/or emotional distress.

## Signs of Mental Health Issues in School-Aged Children (Ages 9–12)

As children enter school age, they are more likely to express their feelings verbally, but they may still struggle with articulating complex emotions. At this age, children are developing social skills, coping strategies, and their sense of identity, so emotional difficulties can often manifest through changes in behavior, social

When children reach school age, they tend to verbalize their emotions but may continue to have difficulty expressing abstract emotions. At this developmental stage children are learning social skills, adaptive strategies, and individual identity, and so emotional problems are often reflected by behavioral, social interactions, or academic performance.

**Behavioral Changes**

1. **Decline in School Performance**: Sudden deterioration in school performance, trouble focusing, or lack of engagement with learning can be an indication that a student is experiencing emotional distress. This could be due to anxiety, depression, or a lack of ability to cope with stress, all of which can impair a child's ability to concentrate or participate in his/her tasks.

2. **Social Withdrawal or Bullying:** Children who once were socially participating may stop participating socially, abstain from group activities, or have difficulty developing and sustaining peer relationships. On the other hand, some children may act out aggressively, either by bullying others or getting into frequent conflicts with peers. Withdrawal and aggressive behavior can both serve as indicators of underlying emotional disturbance such as depression, anxiety, or trauma.

3. **Mood Swings and Irritability:** Another symptom of the risk of mental health disorder is frequent and intense fluctuations in mood, that is, intense highs and lows. Children who appear to have difficulties in emotion regulation can display irritability, sadness, or anger that appears excessive to the circumstances.

4. **Self-Harm or Talk of Death:** In the paediatric age, self-injury, e.g., cutting, preoccupation with death, suicidal thoughts, or hopelessness should never be ignored. These behaviors are red flags that require immediate attention. Although children who

express suicidal thoughts are not necessarily suicidal, such utterances must not be ignored and professional help should be sought.

**Physical Symptoms**

1. **Changes in Sleep or Appetite**: Just as in younger children, school-aged children who are struggling emotionally may experience changes in sleep patterns (insomnia or excessive sleeping) or significant changes in appetite (loss of appetite or overeating). These physical symptoms are also frequently indicative of emotional distress.
2. **Frequent Complaints of Illness:** Children who have a history of complaining habitually of pain in the abdomen, head, and back in the absence of any obvious medical explanation could be suffering from anxiety, depression, or stress.

## Signs of Mental Health Issues in Adolescents (Ages 13–18)

Mental health issues can be amplified in adolescence as adolescents attempt to cope with identity, peer group, and accruing academic and social demands. Adolescents may be more intense about their emotions, but they may also display impulsive behaviors to compartmentalize or cope with, their underlying mental health concerns.

**Behavioral and Emotional Changes**

1. **Extreme Mood Changes**: Adolescents can be subjected to high fluctuations in their emotions caused by endocrine shifts, but if these emotional shifts become extreme or chronic, they may represent the underlying disorder such as bipolar disorder, depression, or anxiety.

2. **Substance Abuse:** Teens who begin using alcohol, drugs, or other substances to cope with stress or emotional pain may be attempting to self-medicate. Substance abuse may also be a manifestation of underlying psychiatric disorders and a means whereby such disorders are further triggered.

3. **Risky Behaviour or Self-Destructive Actions:** Engaging in risky behaviors, such as reckless driving, unsafe sexual activity, or fighting, can be

a sign that an adolescent is struggling with emotional regulation, depression, or feelings of hopelessness. Self-injury, for example, cutting or burning or other self-inflicted physical injuries, is also a severe indicator of psychopathology.

4. **Withdrawal from Family or Friends:** A teen who isolates themselves from family or friends, becomes reclusive, or refuses to engage in activities they once enjoyed is likely struggling emotionally. This withdrawal can be indicative of depression, anxiety, and other psychological disorders.
5. **Expressing Suicidal Thoughts:** Possibly the most alarming feature that indicates a teenager may be suffering from serious mental health problems is the thoughts or intent/plan to die. Teens that discuss death, become hopeless, or mention going away from life require the attention of mental health professionals at once.

# Chapter 3: Causes of the Mental Health Crisis in Children

Identifying the causes of mental health difficulties in children is of paramount importance in the response and prevention of emotional distress with the potential for serious consequences, including self-harm and suicide. Mental health problems (MHPs) among children are typically the result of an interactive effect of biological, environmental, and social factors. These factors can vary from child to child, but recognizing them can provide crucial insight into how we can better support and protect young people.

While no single factor can be pinpointed as the cause of mental health problems, the accumulation of risk factors whether they be genetic, environmental, or social can significantly increase a child's vulnerability. By exploring these contributing causes, we can better equip parents, caregivers, and educators to intervene early and create environments that support mental health and emotional resilience.

## Genetic and Biological Factors

Mental health is underpinned by genetic and biological factors. Children arrive with individual genetic susceptibilities that may affect their ability to regulate emotions and become at risk for psychiatric disease. In some cases, children may inherit genes that predispose them to mental health issues, such as depression, anxiety, or bipolar disorder. Nevertheless, it is not the only factor that will decide whether these conditions will be developed for a child, and other factors are required to be at play.

## Family History of Mental Illness

A family history of mental disorders is one of the most important genetic risk factors for mental health. Adolescents with parents, siblings, and/or close relatives who were treated for psychiatric disorders are also more prone to it (i.e. Research has indicated that mental health disorders, e.g., anxiety, depression, schizophrenia, may be familial, implying a genetic contribution to these disorders.

Yet it is also necessary to know that genetics are only one part of the whole equation. The presence or absence of a family history of mental illness does not guarantee that a child will get a psychiatric disorder, nor the lack of such a family history does it assure the child of immunity. Environmental and social factors are also equally important determinants in the onset of mental health problems.

## Environmental and Social Factors

Although biological factors are the basis of mental health, environmental and social factors are as important as biological factors in the development of a child's emotional health. The environment in which a child develops and finds himself/herself in his/her family, school, community, and in his/her interpersonal relationships can both protect him/her from psychopathology or increase his/her susceptibility to it.

## Early Childhood Experiences and Trauma

One of the most profound environmental influences on mental health is early childhood experiences, particularly trauma. Children who experience abuse, neglect, or other forms of trauma are at a significantly higher risk of developing mental health issues later in life. Traumatic experiences, most acutely during the developmental period, can derail typical brain maturation and affect a child's capacity to modulate emotion, build secure relationships, and adapt to stress.

Trauma may include a variety of types, such as physical, affective, or sexual and/or generalized gonadal abuse, witnessing the abuse of a family member sexually or violently, experiencing any death of, or living with, dependent on familial bonds, a traumatic or disrespectful death of a peer, a traumatic or disrespectful end to a love relationship, or any life with the addictive disease substance abuse or psychiatric illnesses. These negative childhood experiences (ACEs) carry long-term effects and are associated with depression, anxiety, post-traumatic stress disorder (PTSD), and other emotional problems.

The impact of trauma is not always immediately visible. Distress may be apparent in children in forms of aggression and withdrawal, whereas in some the feelings may be internalized, manifesting in forms of depression, anxiety, and self-harm. Negative experiences of childhood should be treated early and the necessary therapeutic interventions should be instituted to allow the child to recover and develop better ways of overcoming crises.

## Family Dynamics and Parenting Styles

Family dynamics and parenting styles are also crucial factors in a child's mental health. Children raised in the context of supportive, affectionate, and continuous parenting are at increased risk of developing healthy emotional regulation and resilience. On the other hand, children raised with inconsistent, neglectful, or abusive parenting can be at increased risk of mental disorders.

Parent-child interactions are of particular importance to the development of emotional well-being. For example, children who feel safe and valued in their relationships with their parents are better equipped to handle life's challenges. However, children raised in environments of lack of being loved, lack of being heard, or in a dangerous environment may have difficulty with inadequateness, fear, or a loss of being seen as valuable.

## Peer Relationships and School Environment

As children grow older, their social interactions with peers and the broader school environment play an increasingly important role in shaping their mental health. It is school years that can be a period of great emotional development, but also very demanding ones. Bullying, social marginalization, academic achievement stress, and peer conflict are all factors that can lead to mental health problems.

Bullying is an especially damaging type of peer assault which can leave a lasting impact on the emotional and psychological well-being of a child. Bullied children are at risk of developing depression, anxiety, and also suicidal thoughts. The isolation, shame, and diminished self-worth associated with bullying can result in significant personal and developmental implications for the victim.

A child's socioeconomic status may have a major effect on his/her mental health. Children growing up in poverty or facing economic hardship are at a higher risk for a range of mental health issues. The anxiety caused by financial vulnerability, lack of access to resources, and opportunity can lead to a sense of helplessness and despair.

Children in lower-income households may also face additional stressors, such as food insecurity, poor housing conditions, or exposure to violence in their communities. Such conditions can engender an unhealthy situation that reaches deep into a child's psych-emotional functioning. Furthermore, families in lower socioeconomic brackets may have less access to mental health care or support services, which can make it more difficult for children to receive the help they need.

## Societal and Cultural Influences

Cultures and societies shape the perception of and response to mental illness. Stigma related to mental illness persists in many cultures and can shame children and their parents into not seeking treatment. Shame and fear of being stigmatized may keep children from disclosing their emotional distress or seeking help.

# Chapter 4: The Road to Crisis

Mental health problems in children do not usually show up immediately. They are usually due to a cumulative effect of emotional, social, and environmental influences. The process by which a child moves from experiencing emotional distress to reaching a crisis point where their mental health severely impacts their well-being can often be invisible to those around them. This chapter will discuss the process by which a child's mental health is lost in time, the signals that should never be dismissed, and how early treatment can change the course of the road towards crisis.

## The Escalation of Emotional Distress

Emotional problems in children particularly if left unaddressed, tend to worsen. From mild symptoms (e.g., irritability, mood instability, or social withdrawal), symptoms may escalate and evolve into more serious mental illness (e.g., anxiety, depression, self-harm behavior). It should be clear that children do not always know how to describe what is bothering them and that at times these discreet changes in behaviour are their only indication that something's not right.

## Denial and Minimisation

Denial of the progression of mental health disorders is a significant bottleneck in their detection. There may be underestimation among children and adults (parents, caregivers, and teachers) concerning first warning signs, and they may consider that the child is 'just going to outgrow it'. This denial may also be due to social stigma to mental health, whereby emotional difficulties are also seen as a sign of imperfection or a problem that will subside by itself.

In children, mental health difficulties may present as what appears "typical" for their age (e.g., mood instability or social avoidance). These behaviors can be attributed to developmental change, for example. Yet when these symptoms continue or get worse with time, they should be given higher priority for treatment. For example, a child who has occasional sadness or frustration may experience an intensification of these emotions as they are unable to process them or get the support they need.

Parents and caregivers must be vigilant and proactive. What is also good to know is that emotional upset is not a "rough patch" that every child experiences, particularly when withdrawal, agitation, and inattention lead to chronic issues.

## The Pathway to Mental Health Crisis

When a child's manifestation of emotional distress makes a deeper development, they may mysteriously show behaviors or symptoms that prompt a psychiatric emergency. The transition from working through emotions to a full-blown mental health crisis may occur over months or even years, however, the process is usually insidious and must not be dismissed.

## Escalating Symptoms of Anxiety and Depression

In children with anxiety or depression, the symptoms can initially be mild but may worsen and escalate to a substantial extent. A child who is anxious about school or social interactions may begin to avoid these situations altogether. This avoidance, if left unaddressed, can lead to social isolation, further deepening feelings of loneliness and sadness. Depression, for example, could arise from disengagement from things they used to like to do or excessive social isolation. With the advancement of depression, emotional numbness, hopeless mood, and loss of the ability to carry out daily activities can occur.

Depression in children can occur differently than in adults. Although sadness is a primary symptom, children may show irritability, anger, or concentration difficulties. They may report physical symptoms like tummy pains or headaches, which can be manifestations of their emotional upset being inappropriately expressed. Untreated, these manifestations can worsen impeding the child's ability to deal with school, relationships, and other aspects of life.

## Self-harm and Suicidal Thoughts

In some children, the pain associated with untreated mental health conditions may take the form of self-destructive behavior. Self-injury, for instance, cutting, burning, or other types of lesions, is widely employed as a means by children to vent or relieve emotional suffering that they are unable to normally cope with. Self-harm is an incredibly dangerous coping mechanism, and it is one of the clearest indicators that a child is in crisis and may be at risk of suicide.

Suicidal ideation, or thoughts of self-harm or death, is another critical sign that a child's mental health has deteriorated to a point of crisis. Children may express their feelings of hopelessness, despair, or worthlessness in subtle ways, such as saying things like "I don't want to be here" or "I wish I could disappear. These comments should never be taken lightly, even if they seem like offhand remarks or cries for attention. This is the case in children suffering from these types of thoughts who are in severe emotional suffering and require prompt intervention.

It should be noted that suicidal ideation in children can sometimes present in a different form compared with adults. In general, especially younger children, it is not always clear what suicide is, but they may convey a sense of wanting to disappear or be done with their pain. With increasing age, children may become more direct in their thinking, and adults should not ignore any suggestion of self-harm.

## The Role of Social Media and Peer Pressure

These days, social media can have a huge impact aggravating a child's mental health disorder. A lot of children are under pressure to post a perfect, airbrushed version of their lives on social media and this can lead to feelings of insecurity, isolation, and anxiety. Cyberbullying is just one other critical problem that can lead to emotional suffering in adolescents.

Children who suffer cyberbullying may feel alienated, disempowered, and unsafe. The consequences of online harassment can be serious, including depression, anxiety, and suicide. Social media platforms can create an environment where children feel constantly judged and compared to their peers, which can increase feelings of isolation and distress.

Other important contributing factors are peer pressure and the need to belong, which play a major role in pushing a child into a crisis. Whether it's the pressure to excel academically, conform to social standards, or engage in risky behavior, children are often influenced by the expectations of their peers. Those who feel like they don't measure up to these social norms may experience deep feelings of rejection, inadequacy, and worthlessness.

## The Importance of Early Intervention

Although a crisis can initiate a long, dark, scary path, early intervention can prevent an otherwise healthy child from sliding into a critical ¬point'. The diagnostic screening of a child's mental health still falters and early intervention well before the issue becomes a crisis has the potential to make a real difference in avoiding adverse outcomes including self-harm or suicide.

**Open Communication**

Okay, the next step in planning for an intervention is developing a safe, interactive, and communicative environment for the intervention. Being open with an adult, parent, school counselor, or counselor about what they are experiencing improves a child's access to the support they need. Open communication provides children with the opportunity to express their problems and this does not lead to crises.

**Professional Support and Treatment**

Clinical intervention by mental health practitioners is nonetheless essential when there is an increase or prolonged presence of symptomatology in a child. Therapists, psychologists, and/or psychiatrists can supply validated tools to address emotion, stress, and coping. In certain contexts, it may be indicated to perform pharmacological therapy to support the clinical management of anxiety, depression, and other psychopathologies of the child.

# Chapter 5: Prevention and Intervention

Particularly, the capacity to prevent mental health issues in children and to intervene early when mental health issues start can have very significant implications on the psychological health of a child. If intervention is caught early, the likelihood of being able to provide a good tool to children to cope with their mental health problems at their early stages, before they reach the crisis level, is maximized. In this chapter, we shall discuss different approaches for prevention and intervention, with particular reference to the need for early detection, expert help, and the development of healthy emotional coping responses.

## Prevention: Building Strong Foundations for Mental Health

Prevention of mental health struggles is a proactive process that starts early in a child's life. That traverses the metaphor of fracture/removal, sand filling and restriction (SMR), nature, art, and sensory, to create an environment that fosters emotional health, healthy interpersonal relations, and strong coping skills. Proactiveness, however, must go hand in hand with developing in children the competencies and tools mediating percept and regulation of affect to limit the risk of developing pathological mental health as an adult life problem.

### 1. Promoting Emotional Intelligence

Emotional intelligence (EI) is the ability to identify, understand, and manage one's own emotions and the emotions of others. If we can encourage EI in children (from a very young age) then we can equip them to have positive emotional attachment and create a resilience to stress and trauma. The ability of children to recognize their own emotions, talk about them, and cope with them in a healthy way as well as the ability to recognize others' emotions, may disable them from developing psychopathology.

### 2. Creating Safe, Supportive Environments

Safety and support are often desired by children in children's homes, schools, and communities. Secure environments promote self-efficacy and security, forming the bedrock of good mental functioning. Parents, carers, and educators can design safe contexts in which to do empathy, nonjudgmental-and-routine strategies. Such environments promote a "talking" culture, in which children are free to voice their thoughts and their souls, unpunished by censure or mockery.

### 3. Encouraging Healthy Lifestyle Habits

Physical health is closely linked to mental health. Motivating children to exercise, eat healthily, and fall asleep can have a great impact on their emotions. Exercise has the effect of producing endorphins, which enhance mood and diminish the sensations of anxiety or depression. Nutrition is important for brain processing, and the quality of sleep is also effective in enabling healthy emotional control and subsequently well cognitive performance.

## Intervention: Responding to Mental Health Struggles

Despite the success of prevention, it is also a reality that, even in ideal circumstances, a certain number of children will go on to become mentally ill. Any time that emotional distress or mental illness is present, early intervention is especially important to prevent the problem from becoming a crisis. This paragraph is a description of the procedure for performing intervention when a child starts to develop symptoms of mental health.

### 1. Recognizing Early Warning Signs

As seen in Chapter 2, the capability to notice some of the early warnings is vital to prevent worsening. When a child reveals behavioral changes, including persistent sadness, social withdrawal, school problems, and behavioral adjustment, these symptoms should always be taken seriously to address them by professionals. Early intervention is a promising ability to help decrease the burden of mental disorders and help instill adaptive coping cognitions in children.

### 2. Seeking Professional Help

Nevertheless, if signs and symptoms of mental health problems are ongoing, this is a subject for professional care. Mental health professionals, for instance, therapists, counselors, or psychiatrists have gone on to become able to assess the situation and provide appropriate therapy. Of a more general nature, therapy in particular can provide the child with a means of escape from distressing thoughts and feelings and, as a consequence, the child will be in a position to learn techniques for dealing with the thoughts and feelings, from the identification of thoughts, feelings and emotions.

### 3. Collaborating with Schools

School is a major demand for children, teachers and school counselors may play a significant role in the detection of mental health crises. It is also possible to train staff to look out for the indicators (e.g., behavioral, school performance, social bonding in the child). Working in partnership with schools and families, children can access additional support in different ways, either through counseling or other assistance, and also be supported by someone they trust.

# Chapter 6: Breaking the Stigma

The stigma surrounding mental health remains one of the most significant challenges for the identification and treatment of mental health disorders in childhood. This stigma does not only delay the drawing near to the rescue of children, but it also encourages children to think that emotional suffering is something that should be ashamed of and that cringing is the result. This chapter will discuss the purpose of stigma about children's mental health, and investigate ways in which stigmatizing barriers can be dispelled so that all children can access the support that is potentially available to them.

## The Power of Stigma

Stigma represents the negative judgments and beliefs of society toward people with psychiatric disorders. This stigma can also take various expressions, such as labeling, stigmatizing, discriminating, and being afraid. Children with mental health conditions tend to perceive themselves as 'weird' or 'wrong' and hence more likely to be pathologized or ostracized by trying to get treatment.

Stigma related to mental health has a terrible effect on children who are, for example, also found to keep their feelings secret, do not seek treatment, and/or suffer in silence. It is also conceivable that children may refuse a diagnosis for the reason they do not wish to be labeled "crazy" or "unwell" and therefore refrain from any treatment. The wish to look "normal" can be extremely stressful for most children, and the likely outcome is conformity with the norm, even to the detriment of their access to the treatment so desperately required.

## The Role of Society

To help overcome the stigma of mental health disorders a cultural change in how we interpret emotional difficulties and psychiatric care is needed. The fact that, in society, mental health deserves as much attention as physical health, and that asking for help is not a mark of weakness, but a mark of strength is of paramount importance. Discussion of mental health should be set as a normal "right" thing and a new narrative should be established against the sense of mental health as a thing to be feared.

## The Role of Parents and Caregivers

The goal of parents/caregivers is to assist the child in overcoming the stigma surrounding mental disorders. By modeling healthy emotional expression, openly sharing about mental health, and looking for support, in turn, parents can offer validation that feeling and getting support is not shameful. As parents approach mental health help in an open, non-intensive manner, the children are prepared to experience these affective states and seek help during the most vulnerable period (Lau, Chang-Chai, and Hsu, 2009).

**Educating the Public**

Education is a key tool in breaking down stigma. Schools, communities, and media have all the potential to influence attitudes towards mental health. By providing education in mental health, emotional health, and strategies to deal with difficult situations, we can play a role in reducing anxiety and misinformation surrounding mental health conditions. Mental health awareness campaigns, mental health awareness activities, and classroom learning are all valuable tools for “destigmatizing “psychotherapy.

# Chapter 7: Tools for Building Emotional Resilience

Emotional resilience is the capacity to deal with stress, adversity, and trauma. The capacity to negotiate life's difficulties and the inherent variability of the natural developmental process of childhood is an important life skill for the developing young person in an attempt to develop emotional resilience in the young adult. In this chapter, we will present the ways and means by which tools and techniques can assist children to build this kind of resilience and emotional resilience to the adversity it will bring.

## Understanding Emotional Resilience

Emotional resilience, though, may not be a childhood constant, but rather, a series of skills that can and will evolve with a given experience. Resilience is defined as the ability to cope with stress and change, and to go through adversity. Emotionally resilient children are more skillful in handling negative affect, controlling levels of stress, and sustaining attention during unpleasant situations.

Attempts to create resilience begin by educating the child that adversity and disappointments are a normal part of life and that it is fine for them to feel the way they do. Through education that shows children that challenges do not have a defining quality and that they can work past challenges, we provide the strength to allow children to develop resilience

**1. Fostering a Growth Mindset**

The development of a growth mindset is one of the most important factors in the development of resilience. A growth mindset is a cognitive attitude that intelligence and related abilities can be developed by hard work, learning, and being tenacious. It is shown that children developing a growth mindset are less likely to see difficulties as a source of failure, but on the contrary as "a learning experience. When children are role-modeled the experience of failure as a "learning opportunity," children become more resilient to adversity.

### 2. Building Social Support Networks

Resilience is also mediated by the (availability of) the social networks of the child. Prosocial skills that come from family, friends, and mentors are useful in preparing children to deal with stressful events. Because there are individuals whom children can rely on, that tends to alleviate that feeling of isolation and opens the way for them to better weather life challenges.

### 3. Teaching Problem-Solving Skills

Resilient children are skilled problem-solvers. They are also able to evaluate context, decision-making, and thus a response. Providing the ability to children to tackle problems can give them the sense of competence and resourcefulness that they need to resolve problems.

Giving children the chance to make decisions and solve problems autonomously, with the necessary support, has a positive impact on their self-esteem and emotional stamina.

# Chapter 8: Advocacy and Systemic Change

Although the task at the individual level to address child mental health is of high significance, the task at the grand scale level in the mental health problem is also unquestionable. Advocacy is the voice of the voiceless, which can give a lot to the improvement of mental health services, reduce stigma, and make sure that all children are provided with what is necessary and what makes sense to better respond to their needs.

## The Need for Systemic Change

Mental health care for children in countries across the globe is frequently inadequately funded, understaffed, and under-resourced to respond to the challenges children face with mental health concerns. In situations of resource scarcity, time spent on waiting lists, reduced access to mental health professionals, and reduced insurance for children for whom it is used, these are the typical impacts.

## Advocating for Policy Change

There is a need for action and advocacy to achieve policy action to enhance mental health treatment for children. Providing children with the support they need is an important part of this process in increasing mental health service spending, access to mental health services, and mental health professionals in schools. Supporters can lobby for legislative and policy enactment to create greater equity in the treatment of the child in the Child mental health system.

# Conclusion

The mental health of children is a high priority, and we need to collaborate to advocate for early intervention, prevention, and support. From understanding the signs and symptoms of mental health issues to breaking down stigma and advocating for systemic change, each chapter of this book has provided tools and strategies for creating a world where children's mental health is taken seriously.

Through the process of emotional resilience building, open communication, and professional support accessibility, we can equip children with a level of emotional power to overcome every challenge life throws at them. By collective action and in consideration of action and compassion, we can strive to provide access to all children to the help and opportunity to grow emotionally and mentally.

Children's
Mental
Mattters

# References

**American Academy of Pediatrics.** (2019). *The importance of mental health in children and adolescents.* American Academy of Pediatrics. https://pediatrics.aappublications.org/content/early/recent

**Centers for Disease Control and Prevention (CDC).** (2021). *Children's mental health.* Centers for Disease Control and Prevention. https://www.cdc.gov/childrensmentalhealth

**National Institute of Mental Health (NIMH).** (2020). *Mental health information for children and adolescents.* National Institutes of Health. https://www.nimh.nih.gov/health/topics/child-and-adolescent-mental-health

**World Health Organization (WHO).** (2018). *Mental health in children and adolescents.* World Health Organization. https://www.who.int/news-room/fact-sheets/detail/mental-health-strengthening-our-response

**American Psychological Association (APA).** (2020). *Mental health and children: A growing concern.* American Psychological Association. https://www.apa.org/news/press/releases/2020/10/mental-health-children

**National Alliance on Mental Illness (NAMI).** (2020). *Mental health issues in children: Early detection and intervention.* National Alliance on Mental Illness. https://www.nami.org/Your-Journey/Kids-Teens-and-Young-Adults

**Ginsburg, G. S., & Silverman, W. K.** (2019). *Treating anxiety in children with cognitive-behavioral therapy: A guide for practitioners.* Guilford Press.

**Reiss, D., & Rutter, M.** (2019). *Childhood stress and its impact on mental health. Journal of Child Psychology and Psychiatry, 60*(3), 232–240. https://doi.org/10.1111/jcpp.13043

**Masten, A. S., & Reed, M. G.** (2019). *Resilience in development: The importance of early intervention. Child Development Perspectives, 13*(1), 47–55. https://doi.org/10.1111/cdep.12298

**Harris, A., & Thompson, J.** (2020). *Breaking the stigma of mental health in children. Child and Adolescent Psychiatry Review, 30*(2), 66–74. https://doi.org/10.1007/s11491-020-09345-3

**Mental Health Foundation.** (2021). *Building emotional resilience in children.* Mental Health Foundation. https://www.mentalhealth.org.uk/publications/building-emotional-resilience-children

**Seligman, M. E. P.** (2018). *Building character and resilience in children. Journal of Positive Psychology, 13*(1), 45–55. https://doi.org/10.1080/17439760.2017.1387083

**Rosen, L. A., & Wiegand, R. R.** (2021). *The role of schools in addressing mental health challenges. The Journal of School Health, 91*(7), 496–504. https://doi.org/10.1111/josh.13035

**Kessler, R. C., et al.** (2018). *Mental health disorders in children: Epidemiology and consequences. Lancet Psychiatry, 5*(2), 124–132. https://doi.org/10.1016/S2215-0366(17)30394-7

**National Institute of Mental Health (NIMH).** (2021). *Mental health treatment and early intervention*. National Institutes of Health. https://www.nimh.nih.gov/health/topics/early-intervention

www.ingramcontent.com/pod-product-compliance
Lightning Source LLC
LaVergne TN
LVHW091124150826
845673LV00002B/964

* 9 7 9 8 2 3 0 5 5 2 0 9 3 *